Viola Time Jog

T0083053

Piano accompaniment book

Kathy and David Blackwell

Teacher's note

These piano parts are written to accompany the tunes in *Viola Time Joggers*. They are an alternative to the viola duet accompaniments or audio tracks, and are not designed to be used with those items. A separate violin piano accompaniment book is available providing parts for when violas play together with violins using *Fiddle Time Joggers*.

Kathy and David Blackwell

OXFORD
UNIVERSITY PRESS

OXFORD
UNIVERSITY PRESS

Great Clarendon Street, Oxford OX2 6DP,
United Kingdom

Oxford University Press is a department of the University of Oxford.
It furthers the University's objective of excellence in research, scholarship,
and education by publishing worldwide. Oxford is a registered trade mark of
Oxford University Press in the UK and in certain other countries

This collection © Oxford University Press 2005, 2013, and 2022

Unless marked otherwise, all pieces (music and words) are by Kathy and David Blackwell and are
© Oxford University Press. All traditional and composed pieces are
arranged by Kathy and David Blackwell and are © Oxford University Press.
Unauthorized arrangement or photocopying of this copyright material is ILLEGAL

Kathy and David Blackwell have asserted their right under the Copyright,
Designs and Patents Act, 1988, to be identified as the Composers of this Work

Database right Oxford University Press (maker)

Impression: 1

All rights reserved. No part of this publication may be reproduced,
stored in a retrieval system, or transmitted, in any form or by any means,
without the prior permission in writing of Oxford University Press

Permission to perform the works in this anthology in public
(except in the course of divine worship) should normally be obtained from
a local performing right licensing organization, unless the owner or the occupier
of the premises being used already holds a licence from such an organization.
Likewise, permission to make and exploit a recording of these works
should be obtained from a local mechanical copyright licensing organization

Enquiries concerning reproduction outside the scope of the above
should be directed to the Music Rights Department, Oxford University Press, at
music.permissions.uk@oup.com or at the address above

ISBN 978-0-19-356226-4

Cover illustration by Martin Remphry

Music and text origination by Katie Johnston
Printed in Great Britain on acid-free paper by
Halstan & Co. Ltd, Amersham, Bucks.

Contents

4

1. Bow down, O Belinda

American folk tune

2. Under arrest!

KB & DB

6

3. Someone plucks, someone bows

Traditional
Words KB & DB

Down, up goes the bow, when we're play-ing fast or slow;

down, up goes the bow, when we're play-ing high or low.

4. Down up

C string special

KB & DB

Down up A string, down up D string, down up G string, down up C string;

Play the D and end with G.

5. Two in a boat

American folk tune

6. London Bridge

English folk tune

I can play my o - pen D,

o - pen G, o - pen D, I can play my

o - pen D, A A D D.

7. Fast lane

KB & DB

Try even faster the second time through!

8. In flight

KB & DB

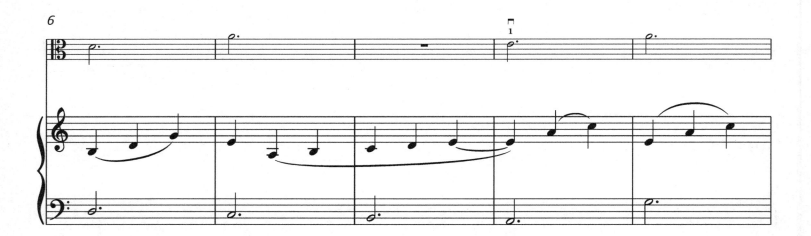

9. Lift off!

KB & DB

10. Katie's waltz

KB & DB

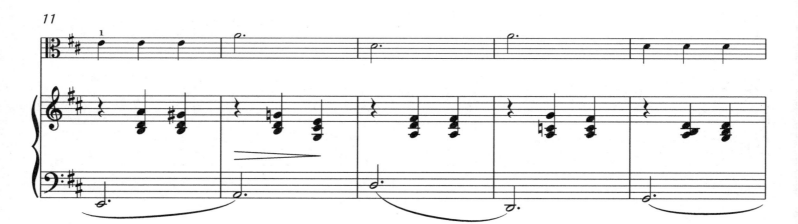

11. Copy cat

KB & DB

12. Tap dancer

KB & DB

13. Rhythm fever

KB & DB

14. Here it comes!

KB & DB

Through the teeth and past the gums, so watch out, tum - my, here it comes!

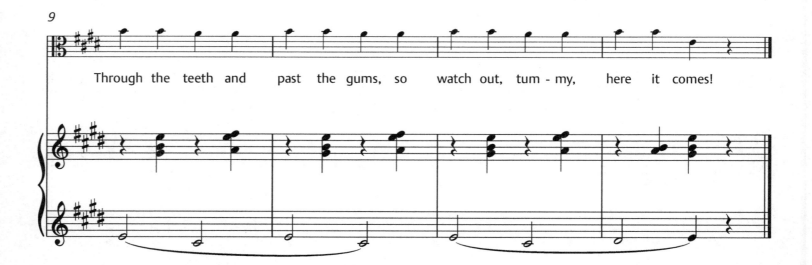

Through the teeth and past the gums, so watch out, tum - my, here it comes!

15. So there!

KB & DB

So there!

cresc.

ff

16. Rowing boat

KB & DB

Gently

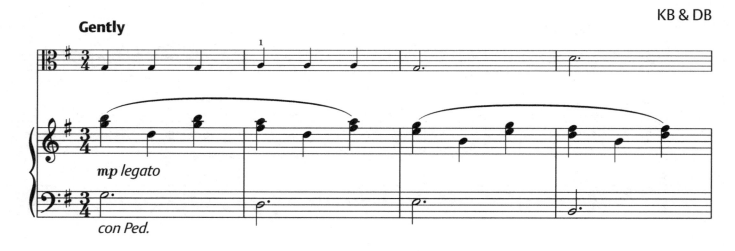

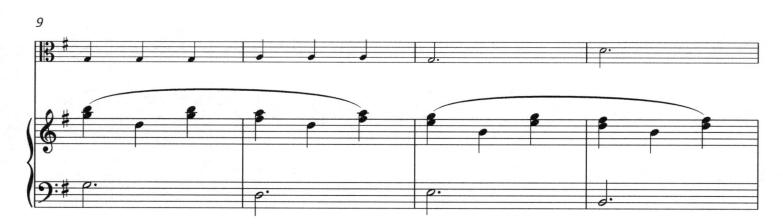

Getting slower

17. Ally bally

Scottish folk tune

18. Tiptoe, boo!

KB & DB

Spookily!

Tip - toe   tip - toe   tip - toe, boo! (*etc.*)

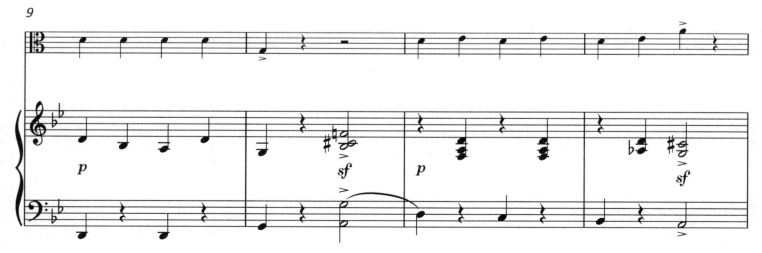

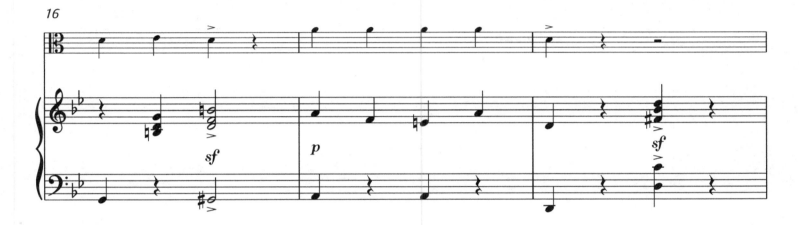

19. Travellin' slow

KB & DB

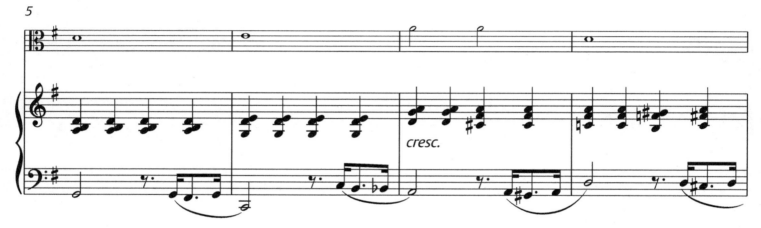

20. C string boogie

C string special

KB & DB

With a gentle swing

* Turn around or, if you are sitting, stand up and sit down again!

21. Off to Paris

French folk tune

23. City lights

KB & DB

Nos. 22 and 23 are reversed to avoid a page turn.

22. Clare's song

KB & DB

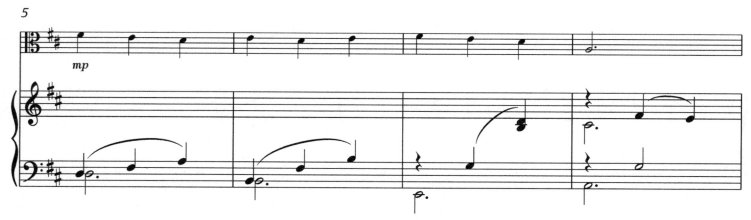

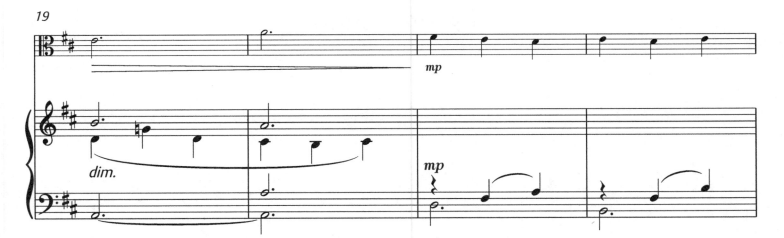

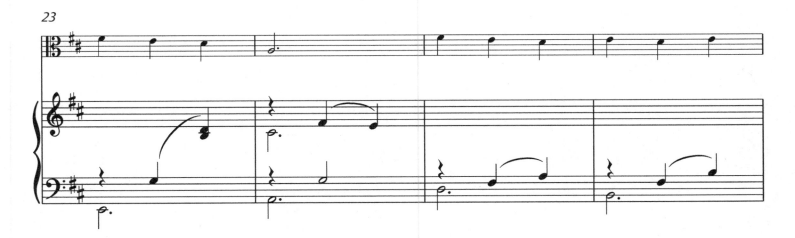

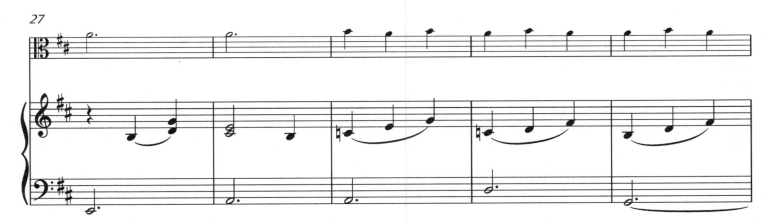

24. Daydream

C string special

KB & DB

25. On the prowl

C string special

KB & DB

With menace

26. Summer sun

KB & DB

27. Phoebe in her petticoat

American folk tune

28. Ready, steady, go now!

KB & DB

29. Cooking in the kitchen

KB & DB

30. Happy go lucky *(for Iain)*

KB & DB

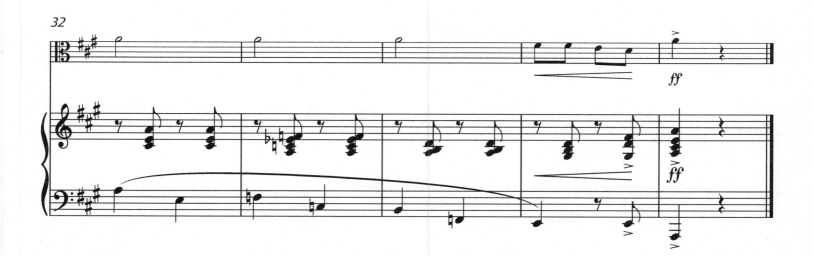

31. The mocking bird

American folk tune

32. Algy met a bear

KB & DB
Words anon.

33. Listen to the rhythm

KB & DB

34. Cattle ranch blues

KB & DB

35. In the groove

KB & DB

36. Stamping dance

Czech folk tune

Heavily

37. Distant bells

KB & DB

38. Lazy scale

KB & DB

Dreamily

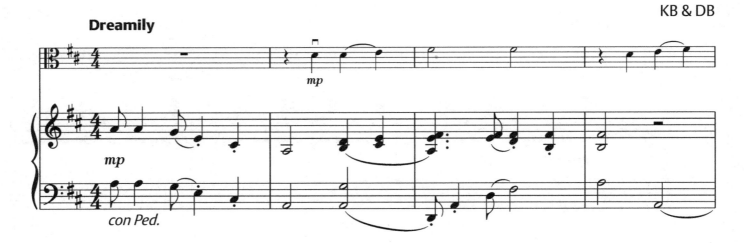

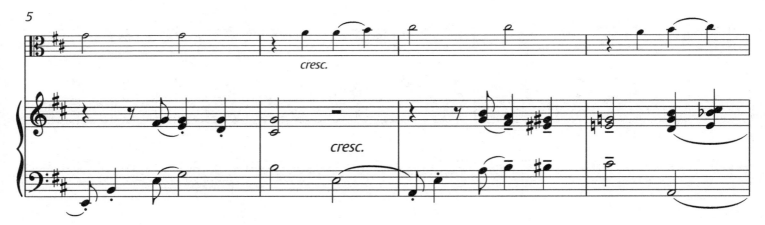

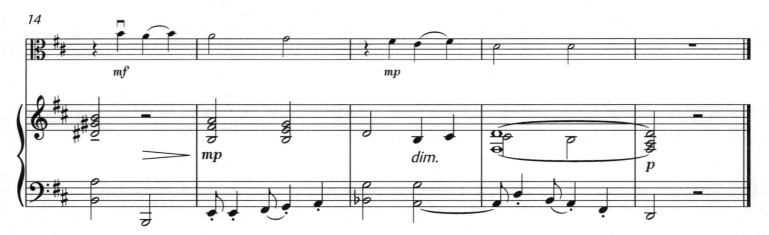

39. Runaway train

C string special

KB & DB

The music is written out in full in the viola part.

40. Rocking horse

KB & DB

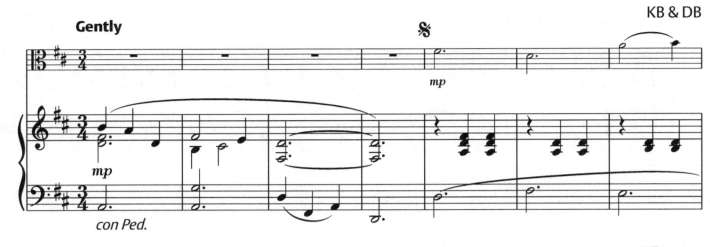

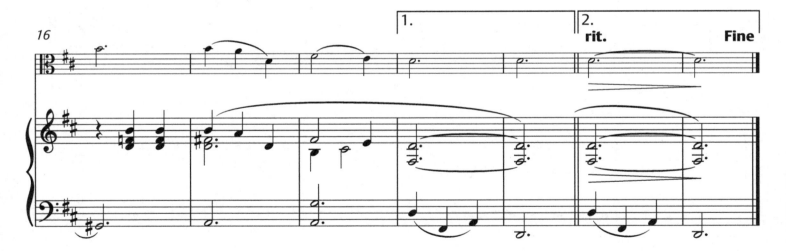

41. Patrick's reel

KB & DB

42. Calypso time

KB & DB

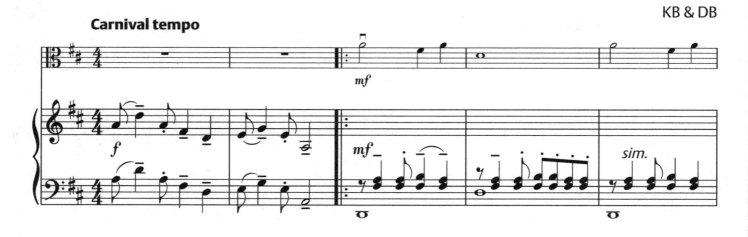

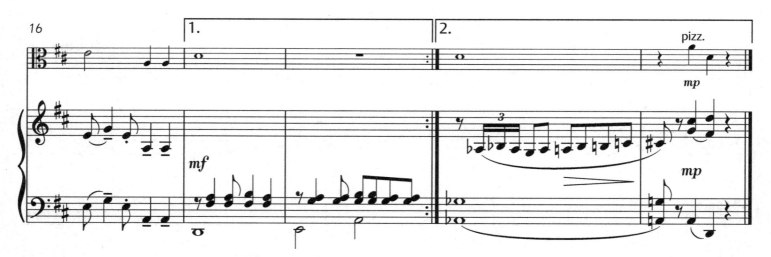

43. Tudor tune

C string special

KB & DB

Lively

44. Chopsticks for two

C string special

KB & DB

45. Carrion crow

American folk tune

47. Viola Time

KB & DB

Easy going

Nos. 46 and 47 are reversed to avoid a page turn.

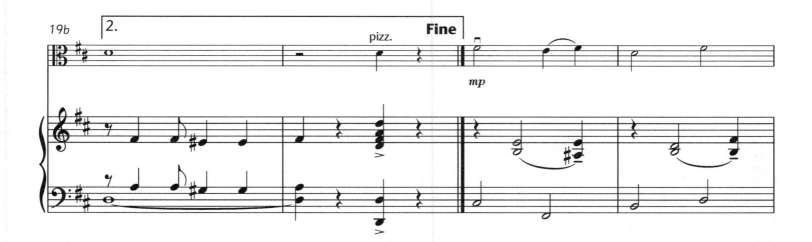

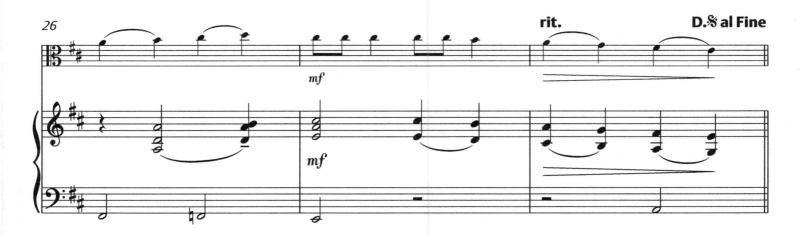

46. *Flying high*

KB & DB

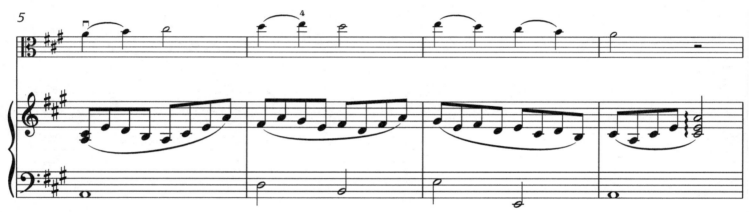

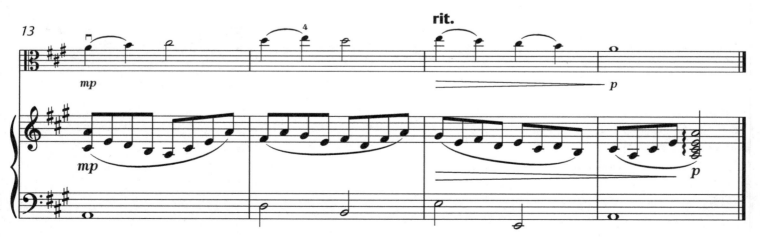